Summer Butterflies

Mila Marquis' ethereal, joyous images are little bliss bombs for the spirit. Her art combines sparkling emotion and unashamedly sweet depictions of fairies, fawns and flowers that cajole even the heaviest spirits to soar. She uses a variety of media, including crayons, coloured pencils, gouache and acrylics, to create her small dreamscapes. There is vast delight to be found in even the smallest of her precious and joy-inducing details.

ISBN: 978-1-4397-7240-9

MIDI FORMAT   144 PAGES   LINED

DESIGNED IN CANADA

Hartley & Marks Publishers Inc. and
Hartley & Marks Publishers Ltd. Made in China.

North America 1-800-277-5887
Europe 800-3333-8005
Japan 0120-177-153

paperblanks.com